THE WORLD OF OCEAN ANIMALS
SEA OTTERS

by Mari Schuh

pogo

Ideas for Parents and Teachers

Pogo Books let children practice reading informational text while introducing them to nonfiction features such as headings, labels, sidebars, maps, and diagrams, as well as a table of contents, glossary, and index.

Carefully leveled text with a strong photo match offers early fluent readers the support they need to succeed.

Before Reading

- "Walk" through the book and point out the various nonfiction features. Ask the student what purpose each feature serves.
- Look at the glossary together. Read and discuss the words.

Read the Book

- Have the child read the book independently.
- Invite him or her to list questions that arise from reading.

After Reading

- Discuss the child's questions. Talk about how he or she might find answers to those questions.
- Prompt the child to think more. Ask: What did you know about sea otters before reading this book? What more would you like to learn?

Pogo Books are published by Jump!
5357 Penn Avenue South
Minneapolis, MN 55419
www.jumplibrary.com

Library of Congress Cataloging-in-Publication Data

Names: Schuh, Mari C., 1975- author.
Title: Sea otters / by Mari Schuh.
Description: Minneapolis, MN: Jump!, Inc., [2022]
Series: The world of ocean animals
Includes index. | Audience: Ages 7-10
Identifiers: LCCN 2021002229 (print)
LCCN 2021002230 (ebook)
ISBN 9781636900728 (hardcover)
ISBN 9781636900735 (paperback)
ISBN 9781636900742 (ebook)
Subjects: LCSH: Sea otter—Juvenile literature.
Classification: LCC QL737.C25 S3385 2021 (print)
LCC QL737.C25 (ebook) | DDC 599.769/5–dc23
LC record available at https://lccn.loc.gov/2021002229
LC ebook record available at https://lccn.loc.gov/2021002230

Editor: Jenna Gleisner
Designer: Michelle Sonnek

Photo Credits: BlueBarronPhoto/Shutterstock, cover; David M Schultz/Shutterstock, 1; David McGowen/iStock, 3; superjoseph/Shutterstock, 4; Kelp Grizzly Photography/Shutterstock, 5; MansonFotos/Shutterstock, 6-7; Minden Pictures/SuperStock, 8-9, 14, 23; Gohier/Visual & Written/SuperStock, 10-11; Danita Delimont/Shutterstock, 12-13; Chase Dekker/Shutterstock, 15; Alan Vernon/Getty, 16-17; Suzi Eszterhas/Minden Pictures/SuperStock, 18, 19; Bob Gibbons/Alamy, 20-21.

Printed in the United States of America at Corporate Graphics in North Mankato, Minnesota.

Dedication: For Sadie, Serafina, and Caruso

TABLE OF CONTENTS

CHAPTER 1

LIFE IN THE WATER

A small group of sea otters floats in the ocean. They rest and sleep in the water.

Sea otters sometimes wrap themselves in **kelp**. Why? This keeps them from floating away.

kelp

Other times, they link paws. This keeps them from floating apart.

Sea otters float in groups called **rafts**. Males and females form separate rafts. Some rafts only have a few otters. Others have around 100!

raft

Sea otters are found in the Pacific Ocean. They mostly live in shallow water and rocky areas along the **coast**. But they sometimes go on land to sleep, **groom**, or care for their young.

TAKE A LOOK!

Where do sea otters live? Take a look!

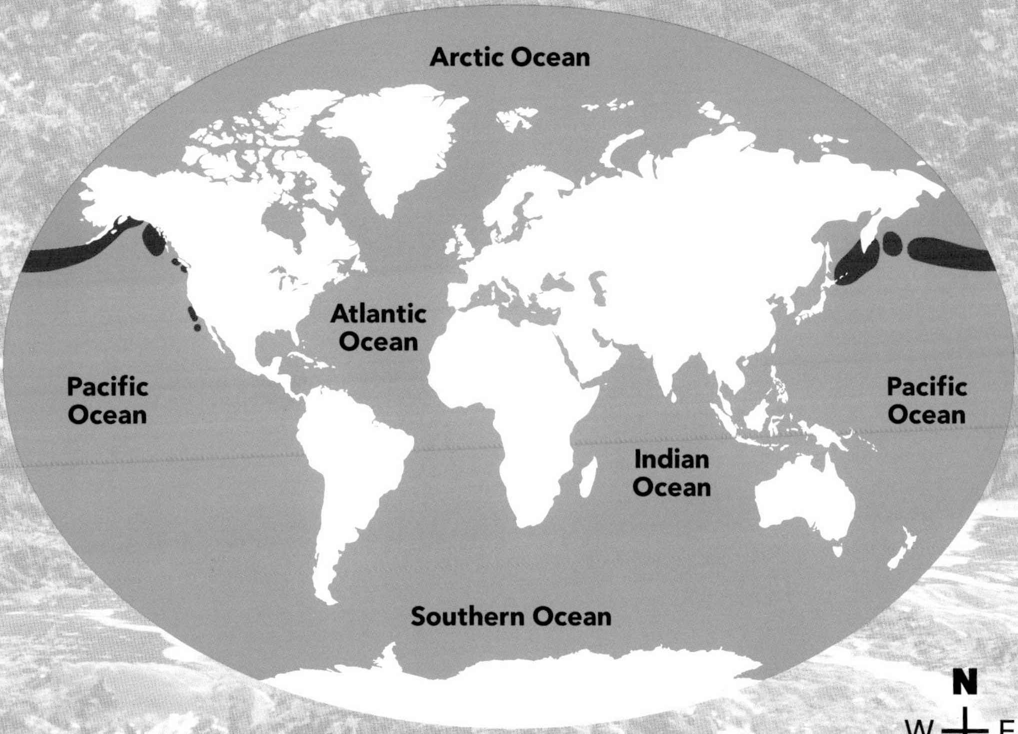

Arctic Ocean

Atlantic Ocean

Pacific Ocean

Pacific Ocean

Indian Ocean

Southern Ocean

N
W ┼ E
S

■ = sea otter range

Sea otters are strong swimmers. Long, flat tails and webbed feet help them swim. Sea otters weigh around 65 pounds (29 kilograms). **Predators**, such as sharks and whales, are much bigger. When danger comes, sea otters quickly swim away.

TAKE A LOOK!

Sea otters are built for life in the water. What are their body parts called? Take a look!

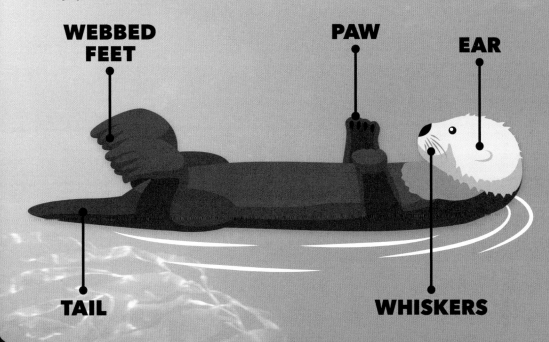

WEBBED FEET

PAW

EAR

TAIL

WHISKERS

Sea otters have very thick, **waterproof** fur. It keeps water away from their skin. It also traps air to keep their bodies warm.

Sea otters groom often to keep their fur clean. This helps it stay waterproof.

DID YOU KNOW?

Sea otters have the thickest fur of any animal!

CHAPTER 2

HUNTING AND EATING

Sea otters are big eaters! They spend a lot of time hunting and eating. They dive to the ocean floor to find food.

Their whiskers feel for **prey**, such as fish and crabs. Clams and snails are good meals, too.

Clams and crabs have hard shells. But sea otters don't let that stop them! While floating on its back, a sea otter will hit the shell on a rock to break it open. Then it's time to eat!

rock

CHAPTER 3

SEA OTTER PUPS

Sea otters are **mammals**. They give birth to live young. Females usually have one **pup** at a time. A coat of soft fur covers the pup. The mother **nurses** and grooms her pup.

pup

A mother carries her pup on her belly as she floats. When she needs to hunt, she wraps the pup in kelp. As the pup grows, its mother teaches it to hunt and swim.

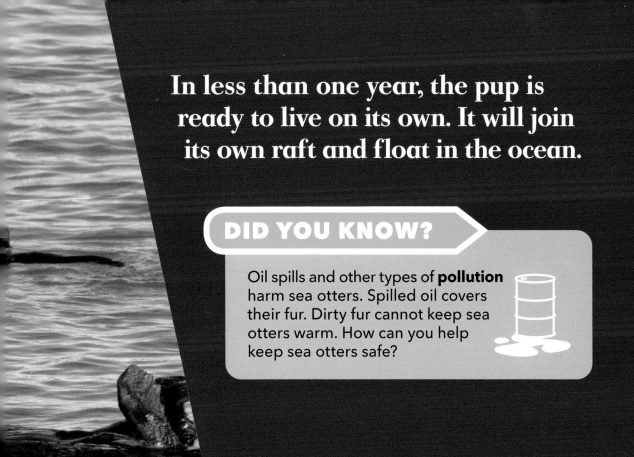

In less than one year, the pup is ready to live on its own. It will join its own raft and float in the ocean.

DID YOU KNOW?

Oil spills and other types of **pollution** harm sea otters. Spilled oil covers their fur. Dirty fur cannot keep sea otters warm. How can you help keep sea otters safe?

ACTIVITIES & TOOLS

FLOAT OR SINK

Sea otters float easily in the water. Learn about floating and sinking with this fun and easy activity.

What You Need:

- a large bowl, bucket, or sink
- small items that can get wet, such as metal utensils, bath toys, corks, coins, rubber balls, keys, foam pieces, or crayons
- towels or paper towels for cleaning up

❶ Have a parent or adult help you fill a large bowl, bucket, or sink with water.

❷ Gather several items that can get wet. Look at the items closely.

❸ Predict which items you think will sink and which items will float. What are your reasons?

❹ One at a time, drop each item into the water. Does it float or sink? Was your prediction accurate?

❺ When you are done, sort the items. Put the items that floated in one pile on a towel. Put the items that sank in another pile on a towel. What did you learn about floating and sinking? Were you surprised?

GLOSSARY

coast: The land next to an ocean or sea.

groom: To take care of and to clean.

kelp: Large brown seaweed that grows in the ocean.

mammals: Warm-blooded animals that give birth to live young, which drink milk from their mothers.

nurses: Feeds a baby milk.

pollution: Harmful materials that damage or contaminate the air, water, or soil.

predators: Animals that hunt other animals for food.

prey: Animals that are hunted by other animals for food.

pup: A young sea otter.

rafts: Groups of sea otters in the water.

waterproof: Does not allow water to enter.

INDEX

TO LEARN MORE

Finding more information is as easy as 1, 2, 3.

① Go to www.factsurfer.com

② Enter "seaotters" into the search box.

③ Choose your book to see a list of websites.

FACT SURFER